# Dear Santa

## Rod Campbell

I wrote to Santa to send me something special for Christmas.

So he wrapped up a . . .

*Too small,* thought Santa.
*I'll send something else.*

So he wrapped up a . . .

*Too big*, thought Santa.
*I'll send something else.*

So he wrapped up a . . .

*Too bouncy, thought Santa.*
*I'll send something else.*

So he wrapped up a . . .

*Too scary*, thought Santa.
*I'll send something else.*

So he wrapped up some . . .

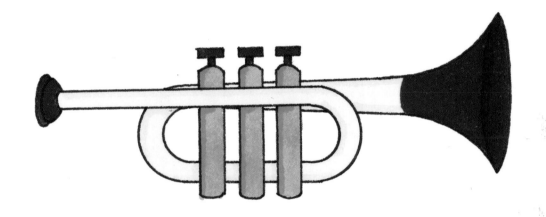

*Too noisy*, thought Santa.
*I'll send something else.*

So he thought very hard,
and on Christmas Eve
Santa brought me a . . .